Motocross Cycles

By A.R. Schaefer

Consultant:
Hugh Fleming
Director, AMA Sports
American Motorcyclist Association

CAPSTONE
HIGH-INTEREST
BOOKS

an imprint of Capstone Press
Mankato, Minnesota

JV JM HB

Capstone High-Interest Books are published by Capstone Press
151 Good Counsel Drive, P.O. Box 669, Mankato, Minnesota 56002
http://www.capstone-press.com

Library of Congress Cataloging-in-Publication Data
Schaefer, A.R.
    Motocross cycles/by A.R. Schaefer.
    p. cm.—(Wild rides!)
    Includes bibliographical references (p. 31) and index.
    ISBN 0-7368-0930-9
    1. Trail bikes—Juvenile literature. 2. Motorcycles, Racing—Juvenile
literature. 3. Motocross—Juvenile literature. [1. Motocross. 2. Motorcycles.]
I. Title. II. Series.
TL441 .S33 2002
629.227'5—dc21   2001000213

Summary: Discusses these racing dirt bikes, their history, parts, and
competitions.

Editorial Credits
Matt Doeden, editor; Karen Risch, product planning editor; Kia Bielke,
    cover and interior designer; Katy Kudela, photo researcher

Photo Credits
ALLSPORT PHOTOGRAPHY, 6–7, 8, 14, 16 (top), 22 (top), 22 (bottom)
Antonio Herrero/Mercury Press, 4 (top), 24
Herb Bersin/FPG International LLC, 12
Isaac Hernandez/Mercury Press, cover, 10 (top), 16 (bottom), 18, 21, 26, 28
Jim Sanderson, 4 (bottom), 10 (bottom), 15

1 2 3 4 5 6 07 06 05 04 03 02

Table of Contents

Learn about:

- **Motocross manufacturers**

- **Motocross events**

- **Motocross classes**

CHAPTER 1

Motocross Cycles

A small yellow motocross cycle speeds over the top of a hill and sails through the air. Dirt flies up behind the cycle's tires as it lands. The rider puts out one foot and makes a sharp turn around a corner. Other cycles follow as the leader rides over a series of bumps. The motorcycle engines make a loud, high-pitched buzz as the riders speed around the track.

Suddenly, the leader loses control on a patch of loose dirt. The cycle slides off the track. Two riders behind the leader crash into one another as they try to avoid the sliding cycle. The rest of the riders steer carefully past the crashed cycles. But in a few moments, all the riders are back on the track. They continue racing to the finish line.

About Motocross Cycles

Motocross cycles are small, powerful
motorcycles that race on dirt tracks. The cycles
are designed to handle well over uneven
ground. Motocross cycles can jump high into
the air. They also can turn and accelerate
quickly. They can reach their top speeds in
only a few seconds.

Many motorcycle manufacturers build
motocross cycles. These companies include
Yamaha, Kawasaki, Honda, and Suzuki.
Manufacturers build cycles for youth and adult
riders. These companies sometimes sponsor

professional riders. They pay the riders to use their cycles or equipment.

Motocross riders take part in a variety of races. These races include outdoor motocross races and indoor supercross races. Each race track is different. Tracks may include different jumps, turns, and bumps.

Most professional motocross racers ride factory bikes. These cycles are slightly different than those sold to the public. Factory bikes may have extra power or better parts. Factory bikes also are more expensive than standard cycles.

Motocross cycles can jump high in the air.

The 250cc is the most popular class of motocross cycle.

Motocross Cycle Classes

Motocross cycles are grouped into classes. Classes are determined by the size of a cycle's engine and the age of the rider. The size of the engine is measured in cubic centimeters (cc). Riders as young as 4 years old may ride cycles with engines as small as 50cc. Older children may ride cycles with 65cc or 85cc engines. Adults may ride cycles with engines as large as 500cc.

The two most common professional motocross cycle classes are 125cc and 250cc. Most major races are for these two classes. Riders of each class race only against riders of the same class. Cycles in the 125cc class are the easiest to control. Their top speed is about 40 miles (64 kilometers) per hour. Cycles in the 250cc class have more power. Their top speed is about 50 miles (80 kilometers) per hour. But the extra engine power makes 250cc cycles more difficult to control.

Many riders begin in the 125cc class. There, they learn the sport and work on their racing skills. They then may move up to the 250cc class. This class is the most popular.

Learn about:

- **Motorcycle scrambles**

- **Husqvarna cycles**

- **Japanese cycles**

CHAPTER **2**

Early Models of Motocross Cycles

The first motorcycles were invented in the late 1800s. They were bicycles with steam-powered engines under the seats. Early cycles could not travel very fast. They only worked well on smooth dirt roads.

Over time, people improved the motorcycle design. They made the tires smaller. They built better engines. These changes made motorcycles faster and easier to ride. People soon began racing motorcycles. But they always stayed on smooth surfaces.

Motorcycle racing became popular during the 1930s and 1940s.

Early Races

One of the first off-road motorcycle races took place in England in 1924. It was called a motorcycle scramble. Other motorcycle scrambles took place during the next 20 years. People began calling them motocross races. This term combined the words motorcycle and cross-country. But few people took an interest in early motocross races.

In 1947, the Motocross des Nations took place in Paris, France. It featured riders from countries throughout Europe. People heard about this race and became interested in motocross racing. The popularity of the sport began to increase in Europe.

U.S. soldiers returned from Europe after World War II (1939–1945). Some of the soldiers had seen the Motocross des Nations and other motocross races. These soldiers told others about the motocross races. The sport began to grow in popularity in North America.

Motocross cycles are built to handle well on rough ground.

Lighter, Faster Cycles

Regular motorcycles could not handle the rough tracks of off-road racing. Riders needed cycles that were built just for motocross racing. The first companies to build motocross racing cycles were Norton and Birmingham Small Arms (BSA). These companies were located in England.

In the 1950s, a Swedish company called Husqvarna built a new motocross cycle. It was lighter, faster, and easier to control than any other cycle at that time. Other motocross cycles could not compete with the Husqvarna model. Other companies soon copied the model.

Motocross cycle design changed again in the 1960s. Japanese manufacturers began making motocross cycles with small, powerful engines. The Japanese cycles were faster and easier to control than other cycles. Japanese companies still make most of the motocross cycles today.

Japanese companies such as Yamaha make most of the motocross cycles today.

Learn about:

- **Prototypes**

- **Engines**

- **Tires**

CHAPTER **3**

Designing a Motocross Cycle

The basic design of a motocross cycle has changed little in recent years. Manufacturers still make lightweight, powerful bikes. Racers may make modifications to their cycles. These small changes slightly affect the way the cycles perform. For example, engine modifications may allow a cycle to reach higher speeds.

Designing a Cycle

New cycle designs begin as prototypes. These cycles are the first working examples of a design.

Test riders try out the prototypes on private tracks. The riders and designers pay close attention to how the prototype performs. They keep the features that work well. They change the features that do not work well.

Pre-production testing is the next step in cycle design. The company builds more cycles based on the prototype testing. These cycles are called pre-production cycles. Riders call them "pre-pros." Many riders try out the pre-pros.

Motocross cycles have two-stroke engines.

They tell the designers which features they like and which they do not like.

The next step in design and testing is the one-off. A one-off is much like the final product. Most one-offs are sold to the public to see how people like them. Designers may then make minor changes to the cycles based on customers' suggestions. But the final model often is the same as the one-off.

Engine

Most motocross cycles have two-stroke engines. These engines have one cylinder and one piston. Fuel is burned inside the cylinder. A spark plug causes the fuel to explode. These explosions cause the piston inside the cylinder to move up and down. This movement provides the cycle's power.

An engine's power depends on its size. Large 250cc engines can burn fuel faster than 125cc engines. Cycles that burn more fuel have higher top speeds.

Tires

Motocross cycles have small, wide tires. A pattern of bumps and grooves called tread stretches around the tire. Tread allows the tire to grip the track.

Riders use different types of tires for different types of tracks. They may use tires with extra deep tread on loose dirt or mud. They may use tires with narrower tread on sand. They may use tires with little tread on hard surfaces.

Other Parts

Riders use a variety of controls to drive their cycles. Three important controls are on the handlebars. They are the brake, the throttle, and the clutch. The rider controls the throttle and the brake with the right hand. The throttle is a twist-grip. The rider turns the grip to increase speed. Riders use the brake to slow down.

The rider controls the clutch with the left hand. Riders must pull the clutch to shift gears. The gear lever is usually under the left foot. On most cycles, the rider presses down on the lever for first gear. The rider pulls the lever up one spot for each higher gear. This gear arrangement is called "one down, four up."

Motocross cycles also have a system of shock absorbers. These devices are attached to the wheels. They help lessen the impact of hard landings. Riders would often be thrown off their cycles without shock absorbers.

Tread helps motocross tires grip the ground.

Learn about:

- Track features

- Events

- Safety

CHAPTER 4

Motocross Cycles in Competition

Most motocross races are for amateur riders. But some riders race professionally. These riders travel around the world to earn their living by racing.

The Track

Most motocross courses are about 2 miles (3.2 kilometers) long. The tracks wind over hills and around trees. No two motocross courses are the same.

Track features include bumps, jumps, and berms. A bump is a small mound of dirt. Larger mounds of dirt are called jumps. Riders may speed over jumps and sail through the air. A sloped pile of dirt on a corner is called a berm. The slope of a berm helps riders turn sharp corners without slowing down.

The Race

Most motocross and supercross races are split into two parts. Each part is called a moto. Each moto includes between five and 10 laps. Most motos take 15 to 20 minutes to complete.

Motocross and supercross tracks include dirt bumps, jumps, and turns.

The same riders compete in both motos. They earn points in each moto depending on their finish. The first-place rider gets one point. The second-place rider gets two points. Riders get more points the lower they finish. The rider with the lowest point total at the end of both motos is the winner.

Organized Racing

Professional motocross riders may race in a series. A series is a group of motocross events. Riders earn points for each event depending on their finish. The rider with the best point total at the end of the series is the winner.

The World Championship Motocross Series is the most popular professional motocross series. The world's top riders compete in this series. Most of the events are held in Europe. The races often appear on TV networks around the world.

The American Motorcyclist Association (AMA) holds professional and amateur motocross events in the United States. The

All motocross racers wear safety gear
such as helmets and gloves.

Canadian Motorcycle Association (CMA) holds motocross events in Canada.

Safety

Safety is important to motocross riders. Crashes are common in motocross events. Riders try to make sure they will not be seriously hurt during crashes.

All motocross racers wear protective gear. They wear helmets with face protectors. They also wear gloves, boots, and light body armor. This strong padding protects a racer's body during serious crashes.

Motocross riders also practice good judgment. They learn how far and high they can safely jump. They understand exactly how their cycles will perform under different track conditions. Riders ride their cycles differently according to these conditions. For example, they may slow down more for corners if the track is wet and muddy. These safety measures help riders enjoy their sport without getting hurt.

Jeremy McGrath

Jeremy McGrath is known as the "king of supercross." He is the most famous and successful racer in supercross history.

McGrath was born November 19, 1971, in San Francisco, California. He began racing BMX bikes when he was 10. He switched to motocross cycles at age 14.

McGrath began racing as a professional in 1988. In 1996, he won 14 of the 15 supercross events he entered. He won 13 of these events in a row. McGrath has won the AMA 250cc Supercross Championship seven times.

McGrath also competes in outdoor events. In 1995, he won the AMA 250cc Motocross Championship. He was on the winning U.S. team in the Motocross des Nations in 1993 and 1996.

Words to Know

berm (BURM)—a banked turn or corner on a motocross track

clutch (KLUHCH)—a lever that a motocross rider must pull in order to shift gears

cylinder (SIL-uhn-dur)—a hollow tube inside an engine in which fuel explodes to create power

modify (MOD-uh-fye)—to change; people modify a vehicle or engine in order to make it faster or more powerful.

prototype (PROH-tuh-tipe)—the first produced version of a new design or invention; riders test prototype cycles to see how well they work.

throttle (THROT-uhl)—a grip or lever that controls how much fuel and air flow into an engine; a motocross rider turns the throttle to speed up.

tread (TRED)—a series of bumps and deep grooves on a tire; tread helps tires grip surfaces.

To Learn More

Freeman, Gary. *Motocross.* To the Limit.
   Austin, Texas: Raintree Steck-Vaughn, 2001.

Hendrickson, Steve. *Supercross Racing.*
   Motorcycles. Mankato, Minn.: Capstone
   Books, 2000.

Young, Jesse. *Motocross Racing.* MotorSports.
   Mankato, Minn.: Capstone Books, 1995.

Useful Addresses

American Motorcyclist Association
13515 Yarmouth Drive
Pickerington, OH 43147

Canadian Motorcycle Association
P.O. Box 448
Hamilton, ON L8L 1J4
Canada

Cycle News World Headquarters
P.O. Box 5084
Costa Mesa, CA 92626

Internet Sites

The Canadian Motorcycle Association
http://www.canmocycle.ca

Motocross.com
http://www.motocross.com

Official Jeremy McGrath Site
http://www.nacnac.com/main.asp

Index